FROM SOUTH DEVON TO THE SOUTH POLE

Plymouth-born Captain Robert Scott (aged 33), recently arrived in Antarctica aboard 'Discovery' in 1902. This was the first pioneering polar expedition he led, called the British National Antarctic Expedition. He is wearing skis and holding a single ski stick. Two sticks were not used until later. The expedition ship is in the background. (Plymouth City Museum)

FROM SOUTH DEVON TO THE SOUTH POLE

PLYMOUTH AND DEVON'S CONNECTIONS WITH THE HEROIC AGE OF ANTARCTIC EXPLORATION (1901-22)

PAUL DAVIES

Paul Davies (signature)

KINGSBRIDGE BOOKS
IN ASSOCIATION WITH THE UNIVERSITY OF PLYMOUTH

Published by Kingsbridge Books
Horswell Coach House
South Milton
Kingsbridge
Devon
TQ7 3JU
www.kingsbridgebooks.co.uk

in association with the University of Plymouth PL4 8AA

For Rob and Alex

ISBN: 978-0-9567472-0-4

Cover, map and expedition page design by Tim Burr
Background cover photo by Peter Paisley
Front cover photo: The *Quest* departing from Plymouth Sound, 1921
(*The Graphic* From a private collection)
Rear cover photo: Detail of the Scott Memorial, Devonport, by Tim Burr

Printed by Nick Walker Printing, The Old Workhouse,
          Higher Union Road, Kingsbridge, Devon TQ7 1EQ

Contents

FOREWORD BY
SIR RANULPH FIENNES

For too long many of the ordinary seamen and scientists who supported Robert Scott and Ernest Shackleton on their epic exploring Antarctic adventures have been overlooked. This book goes some way to rectifying this oversight by turning the spotlight on some of the men who were recruited to sail with them and who performed vital roles during the expeditions. And, all of those featured here have particular connections with Plymouth and the County of Devon. For example, TV Hodgson carried out pioneering marine biological research during the *Discovery* expedition; Francis Davies, the ship's carpenter, worked tirelessly in his responsibility to erect Scott's base hut at Cape Evans; Petty Officer Frank Browning suffered terribly during the sledging expedition but was a stalwart member of the *Terra Nova* Northern Party, and First Officer Lionel Greenstreet stoically endured the hardship of life marooned on Elephant Island when the *Endurance* sank. All these men (and others covered in this book) had strong local connections and their contributions should all be celebrated.

This book also provides fascinating details about some Devon landmarks and monuments that have links with the Heroic Age of Antarctic Exploration. Readers are encouraged to discover for themselves these hidden local connections with polar expeditions. Discovering these local connections should inspire further reading and study.

Together these two strands of research provide a novel and rewarding approach to this inspiring period of Antarctic exploration, and this book rightly celebrates the contribution Plymouth and Devon made to these pioneering expeditions.

Sir Ranulph Fiennes, Exmoor December 2010

vii

Towns in Devon mentioned in this book.

Note about measurements

Explorers at the time would have used imperial measurements and these have been used in this book.

Conversions are as follows:

1 statute mile (or 0.87 nautical mile) = 1.6 kilometre

1 nautical mile (or 1.15 statute mile) = 1.85 kilometre

1 foot = 0.3048 metre

1 pound (1lb) = 0.453 kilogram

1 (UK) ton = 1,016 kilograms

INTRODUCTION FROM THE VICE-CHANCELLOR OF THE UNIVERSITY OF PLYMOUTH, PROFESSOR WENDY PURCELL

We are inspired by, indeed shaped by, the people, the places and the world around us. The University of Plymouth motto - *Explore, Dream, Discover* - captures our ambitions and reflects our location and history of seeking out new things.

Universities are places of discovering new knowledge and Plymouth is a City defined by its spirit of discovery. It has its origins as a major port; and our history revolves around the sea and seafarers. Indeed, the name of Plymouth is explicitly linked with explorers – such as, Sir Francis Drake and Sir Walter Raleigh. And, the Pilgrim Fathers who set off on the Mayflower to establish new communities in America. Captain James Cook set sail from the Plymouth Sound to explore the southern continent. And Robert Falcon Scott, 'Scott of the Antarctic', was born here in Plymouth.

For us, in Plymouth, we are greatly influenced by our natural heritage. Our history as a University is deeply rooted and entwined with that of the City of Plymouth. Our coastal location, deepwater estuary and natural harbour meant it was an obvious place to establish the Plymouth School of Navigation in 1862. And from this humble beginning the University of Plymouth has grown to be a large and successful institution.

While many things have obviously changed since 1862, our commitment to all things Marine and Maritime has not. The University now enjoys a world class presence in these and many other subjects – and we are keen to explore new opportunities and new partnerships. One hundred years ago, Scott began his historic expedition to the South Pole, taking with him many local seamen and scientists. His achievements, and those of his men, are an inspiration to us all and strongly reflect our motto, our need to explore new places, and discover more about the world around us.

Wendy Purcell

Professor Wendy Purcell December 2010

The aim of this book is to show the connections Plymouth, Torquay and South Devon have with the Heroic Age of Antarctic Exploration. Several men who sailed south with Captain Scott and Ernest Shackleton came from this area and there are a number of landmarks and memorials located here. Many have not been written about before and most of the landmarks can still be visited and explored today. Wherever possible, postcodes are given to aid in finding their location using satellite navigation.

A BRIEF HISTORY OF THE BRITISH EXPEDITIONS OF THE HEROIC AGE OF ANTARCTIC EXPLORATION (1901-1922)

The great Southern Continent of Antarctica remained unexplored land at the beginning of the twentieth century. The fiercely inhospitable climate and the treacherous oceanic pack ice around Antarctica prevented any serious exploration of the continent.

Although a number of attempts were made to explore the continent in the closing years of the nineteenth century (most notably by the Norwegian Henryk Bull in 1895, the Belgian Adrien de Gerlache in 1898 and the Norwegian Carsten Borchgrevink in 1899), it was a British expedition led by Plymouth-born Captain Robert Scott at the very start of the twentieth century which was most successful. Backed by both the Royal Geographical Society and the Royal Society, this expedition was called the National Antarctic Expedition and its primary function was science. The ship used was purpose-built in Dundee for scientific exploration and took the famous name *Discovery*.

During the period called the Heroic Age many expeditions set forth, including ones from Germany, Sweden, France, Scotland, Norway, Japan and Australia. They had varying degrees of success. In order to give a background context to the Devon men and landmarks in this book, the expeditions referred to are summarised below.

THE *DISCOVERY* EXPEDITION 1901-4
LED BY ROBERT FALCON SCOTT

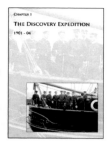

This expedition provided the template for the organisation of most subsequent expeditions. A number of top scientists were included and much pioneering work was carried out. Extensive data on magnetism, meteorology, marine biology and geology were gathered. The men spent two winters in Antarctica and built a hut on shore. They used a hydrogen balloon to go aloft and inspect the ice shelf. Scott led two men, Dr Edward Wilson and Ernest Shackleton, on a three month sledging journey using dogs and man hauling to 82° 16' South; a farthest south record at the time. All suffered from exhaustion and frost bite, and Shackleton suffered the severest scurvy. One man, Able Seaman Vince, was lost in a fall over a precipice during a snow blizzard in the early days ashore. Much was learnt from these experiences which was of great benefit to later expeditions.

THE *NIMROD* EXPEDITION 1907-9
LED BY ERNEST SHACKLETON

Shackleton, it is said, was spurred by his disappointment at being invalided home from the *Discovery* Expedition to lead his own expedition south. He received backing from some wealthy businessmen and again took a team of eminent scientists with him. From the hut they constructed at Cape Royds, one team set out to climb the nearby active volcano Mount Erebus, another to reach the South Magnetic Pole and a third team led by Shackleton himself tried to reach the South Pole. He pioneered the use of ponies for much of the haulage work. After climbing the crevassed Beardmore Glacier they managed to trek for another 20 days across the polar plateau before Shackleton famously made the decision to turn back 97 nautical miles from the Pole in order to save the lives of his now starving men. They only just made it back.

THE *TERRA NOVA* EXPEDITION 1910-13 LED BY CAPTAIN ROBERT SCOTT

This expedition again had dual aims - scientific work and to be first to reach the South Pole. Exploring teams of sledgers went out from the hut at Cape Evans in several directions. Many made spectacular discoveries and had gruelling experiences. Scott's team headed for the South Pole supported by other teams, using dogs and ponies, which laid supply depots. He was famously beaten to be the first to reach the South Pole by a very well organised Norwegian team led by Roald Amundsen. On his return journey from the Pole Scott suffered uncommonly severe Antarctic weather and, through lack of food, all the team of five men perished. The last three were just 11 nautical miles short of a food depot. Scott and his men became national folk heroes at a time of great suffering in Britain during the First World War.

Two Player's Cigarette cards showing the Norwegian Roald Amundsen's successful expedition to be the first to reach the South Pole on 14 December 1911; a month before Scott arrived there.

THE *ENDURANCE* EXPEDITION 1914-17 LED BY SIR ERNEST SHACKLETON

With the South Pole reached, Shackleton planned a new ambitious expedition to cross the continent overland from the Weddell Sea to the Ross Sea via the South Pole, which he named the Imperial Trans-Antarctic Expedition. The expedition was unable to reach the shore as the ship *Endurance* was trapped in the Weddell Sea ice, then eventually crushed and sank. Shackleton inspired his men to survive by first leading them over the ice and then in small boats to Elephant Island. Here most of them stayed for four winter months sheltering under two upturned boats in the harshest of conditions with the bare minimum to survive. Shackleton then miraculously sailed the 22 foot whaler *James Caird* across 800 nautical miles of the roughest ocean in the world to South Georgia to raise the alarm. This he did, and in August 1916 he accompanied a rescue boat to retrieve the 22 stranded men on Elephant Island. In 1917, he accompanied the rescue ship which reached the Ross Sea Party which was awaiting his overland arrival across the continent.

THE *QUEST* EXPEDITION 1921-22 LED BY SIR ERNEST SHACKLETON

Shackleton undertook his last expedition when he was not a well man. He assembled a crew from some of his old comrades who willingly accompanied him south again. The ship *Quest* was unreliable and the aim of the expedition was far from clear. On arriving at South Georgia he took to his cabin and suffered a heart attack and died on 5 January 1922. On his wife's instructions he was buried in the island cemetery. The expedition and its scientific work continued until the ship returned to Plymouth in September 1922.

The focus of this book is Antarctic exploration in the early part of the twentieth century, but there are some other notable south Devon memorials and connections to polar exploration from earlier periods which can be explored.

These include:

- Blue plaques in Dartmouth to John Davis (sixteenth century explorer of the North West Passage) and Sir Humphrey Gilbert (sixteenth century explorer who advocated finding the North West Passage to China) Postcode: TQ6 9BH

- A tablet on the house of William Cookworthy on Notte Street in the Barbican, Plymouth noting that Captain James Cook stayed there before he set sail on his first voyage in 1768   Postcode: PL1 2AZ

- The headstone of Tobias Furneaux in Stoke Damerel Church graveyard, Plymouth PL1 5QL. Tobias Furneaux commanded the *Adventure* as part of Captain James Cook's second voyage of exploration (1772-5) and lived on the Swilly estate in Plymouth, adjacent to Captain Scott's boyhood home at Outlands PL2 3BZ

- A figurehead of Lady Franklin on the boat house at Bantham Quay, near Kingsbridge TQ7 3AN. This came from one of the missionary ships she funded as a memorial to her husband Sir John Franklin, who was lost exploring the North West Passage in 1847.

Figurehead of Lady Franklin at Bantham Quay, near Kingsbridge

THE DISCOVERY EXPEDITION

1901 - 04

OFFICERS AND SCIENTISTS ABOARD 'DISCOVERY'
AT LYTTELTON, NEW ZEALAND (SPRI)

THE PLYMOUTH MARINE BIOLOGICAL ASSOCIATION: WORK PLACE OF SCIENTIST T V HODGSON WHO CONDUCTED PIONEERING RESEARCH ON THE *DISCOVERY* EXPEDITION

POSTCODE: PL1 2PB

The Marine Biological Association on Plymouth Hoe, opened in 1888. Both, E W Nelson (Terra Nova) and R S Clark (Endurance) were also recruited from the staff of the MBA.

Although a native of Birmingham Thomas Vere Hodgson made Plymouth his home. Working first in a bank he studied biology in his spare time and became so accomplished that, in 1895, he was appointed as the Director's assistant at the Marine Biological Association's laboratories in Plymouth, where he became a much respected scientist and academic author. He was then appointed as the first curator of the City Museum, housed in Beaumont House, and it was from here he was given leave to join Captain Scott's *Discovery* Expedition as official biologist.

Well wrapped, against the cold, Hodgson on his round checking the fish traps for specimens by RW Skelton (SPRI)

Nicknamed 'Muggins' on board ship, all comment on his reserve and indefatigable appetite for research. The method he used to gather specimens from under the ice was to cut two holes through it, often near a seal hole and link the two holes with a slot. The wire attached to the dredge would then be dragged between the two. One of the results which fascinated Hodgson was when he discovered a ten legged sea-spider – before then every example had eight. Hodgson was 'constantly busy pickling the shrimps and fish that came up every time the trap is hauled up. His cabin is a crowd of bottled and pickled crustaceans, and he is always at work', recorded fellow naturalist Dr Edward Wilson on 23 May 1902. Hodgson, with Ernest Shackleton, was one of the four men who were considered for return to England for medical reasons after the first season but, as he was not expected to lead a sledge party, was allowed to stay. Interestingly, he wrote that he was aware of the way in which Shackleton was being treated by Captain Scott, hinting at a disagreement between the two men.

MUGGINS

Muggins cartoon from the South Polar Times Vol. 1

Hodgson did have the privilege of accompanying Dr Edward Wilson on one of the last sledge short expeditions in November 1903 around Ross Island. This was to pursue Wilson's quest to discover more about the breeding of Emperor penguins and to collect geological samples. From this trip Wilson was able to conclude that the emperor chicks had a very fast rearing period of just four months, from July to November. It formed the foundation of Dr Wilson's later famous winter journey to Cape Crozier during the *Terra Nova* expedition, which became known as the 'Worst Journey in the World'.

Hodgson appears to have become disgruntled about the extent of the marine biological work he was able to undertake on the voyage to and from the Antarctic. He was somewhat critical of the opportunities he was given for trawling for specimens, complaining that Scott was so capricious that they did not know what was to be done until five minutes beforehand.

On his return to Plymouth from the expedition he was responsible for the development of the City Museum's collections and worked conscientiously on the publication of the expedition's scientific results, especially those relating to marine biology. He became the recognised authority on *Pycnogonida* and *Isopoda*.

Hodgson, however, did not enjoy good health and, though he continued to work at his Plympton home until the end, he died at the age of 64 in 1926. Cape Hodgson, the north point of Black Island in the Ross Archipelego, is named after this Plymouth man. His obituary in the Devonshire Association journal said: 'Hodgson was an untiring and unselfish worker, …For him it was enough that the work was done, he ignored the virtues of self-advertisement. A certain brusqueness was a defensive mask of his shyness, …'

Hodgson's grave in Plympton
St Mary's Churchyard,
PL7 1QW.
He died on 2 May 1926

"Highfield"
TV Hodgson's home in
Plympton.
(John Boulden)

4

THE GRAVE IN FORD PARK CEMETERY, PLYMOUTH, OF FREDERICK DAILEY, THE CARPENTER ON *DISCOVERY*

POSTCODE: PL4 6NT

Hidden away in a Plymouth cemetery in the centre of the City is this grave to Lieutenant Commander F E Dailey, who served as warrant officer and chief carpenter on Scott's first expedition to the Antarctic (the *Discovery* Expedition). In recent years Ford Park cemetery has been maintained by an enthusiastic group of volunteers organised as a trust, and this grave is recognised by them as one of the most notable. Coincidentally, the house where Dailey and his family lived, 22 Devon Terrace PL3 4JD, still stands just beyond the wall of the cemetery, 100 metres from where he is buried.

Fred Dailey's headstone in Ford Park Cemetery which includes the inscription 'Duty Well Done-Deeds not Words
Discovery Scott's Expedition 1901 to 1904'

Fred Dailey served his seven-year shipbuilding apprenticeship in Devonport Dockyard. Scott commended Dailey for the "zealous care" with which he worked during the expedition, recognising the critical importance of his role in maintaining the ship in good order. He was also responsible for erecting the sectional hut which was built ashore for a storehouse and occasional shelter.

5

On board 'Discovery': second from left Fred Dailey with Edgar Evans and George Vince. Vince died on the Discovery Expedition and Evans died with Scott after reaching the South Pole (Discovery Point Museum)

Scott, in his diaries, also mentions Dailey for his work with Ernest Shackleton in devising and constructing an experimental form of sledge, supported on two rum barrels as wheels. He commented '…this machine was soon neglected and forgotten, but…I am sure that for many purposes a very light cart with broad-tyred wheels would have been extremely useful'. Dailey was a member of four sledging parties and the small Dailey Islands in McMurdo Sound were named after him. After a distinguished war career when he was awarded the DSC, he became Barrack Master at the RN Barracks in Devonport.

The contribution to the *Discovery* expedition for which Dailey is perhaps best remembered is for the construction of the wooden memorial cross to Able Seaman George Vince who died in the early days of reaching Antarctica. In March 1902 one of the first sledging parties was sent out from the base with the aim of reaching Cape Crozier. After seven days the weather suddenly changed and a blizzard hit. One man, Clarence Hare, went missing. In very poor visibility they found themselves on an ice ridge. Their boots could not keep a grip. Their leader suddenly saw he was within a step of a high precipice above the sea. In an instant, wrote Scott: '…Vince, unable to check himself in his soft fur boots, shot from among them, flashed past the leader,

6

and disappeared.' This loss severely shocked the entire expedition but from it they learnt some invaluable lessons. Miraculously, the 18-year-old Hare later walked back to the ship after being covered by snow for 36 hours and without warm food for 60 hours!

The memorial cross to Vince, built by Fred Dailey, was erected on the hilltop above Hut Point, and Scott wrote '... it was erected..., so firmly that I think in this undecaying climate it will stand for centuries'. It still stands there today.

Vince's cross (D. L. Harrowfield)

Discovery Crew at Lyttelton, New Zealand 1901by J J Kinsey
George Vince is on the extreme left, standing on the mizzen
Boom,and, Fred Dailey is sitting second from right (SPRI)

Captain Scott's *Discovery* Sledging Flag, Exeter Cathedral

POSTCODE: EX1 1HS

Captain Scott's sledging flag from the *Discovery* expedition hangs in Exeter Cathedral. It has, not surprisingly, faded somewhat. The upper portion was originally yellow and the lower portion dark blue with the Cross of St George by the lanyard. The animal depicted is a stag with antlers and the motto reads 'Ready, Aye Ready'

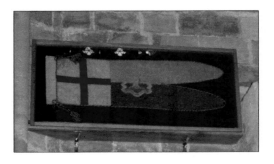

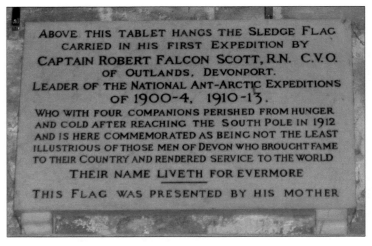

Scott's sledging flag from the Discovery Expedition on the south wall of the nave of Exeter Cathedral, presented by his mother as a memorial to him following his death in 1912. She presented the flag to the Cathedral as Scott was born in Devon.

Flags were a traditional part of sledging in the polar regions dating back to the time of the Victorian explorers, such as William Parry and Sir John Franklin. They clearly had a practical application but their design was also a source of great pride amongst the officers and scientists and a memory of home. According to the diary of Frank Debenham, a geologist on Scott's Last Expedition, each officer of the shore party was expected to have a sledge flag. The usual design was a pennant shape, about two and a half feet long and one foot wide. The square nearest the lanyard was filled with either the Cross of St George or the Union Jack; the rest of the flag consisting of family colours with the family crest. The flags were regularly used as decoration in the hut on high days and holidays.

Christmas day camp 1902 by RF Scott (SPRI)

Scott's *Discovery* flag is shown here on the Southern Journey when they reached the farthest south of 82° 16' South. The photograph was taken on Christmas Day 1902 by Scott (the rope to operate the camera shutter can be seen in his hand). Scott's flag is the middle one of the three; Ernest Shackleton's square flag is on the left, and Dr Edward Wilson's on the right.

Scott's sledging flag from South Polar Times Volume 1

Scott's Discovery Expedition was truly pioneering. He took the latest equipment available, including a hydrogen-filled captive balloon from the Aldershot Balloon Factory. On arrival on the Great Ice Barrier, an ascent in the balloon was arranged for 4 February 1902. The first to make an ascent was Captain Scott and the balloon reached seven hundred feet, so that much previously unseen land could be viewed.

An anonymous article in the South Polar Times about the ascent prophetically said: 'It would perhaps be rash to say anything about the future of ballooning in the polar regions, for when we once reach civilization, we may find flying machines en route to the Poles.' (SPRI)

THE NIMROD EXPEDITION

1907 - 09

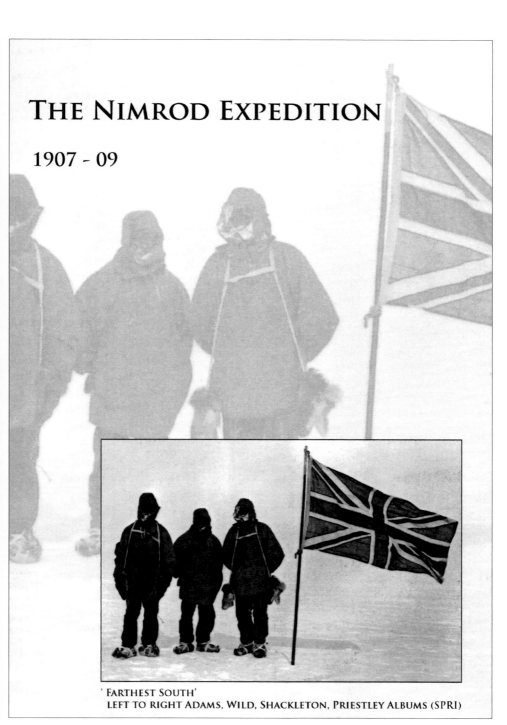

' FARTHEST SOUTH'
LEFT TO RIGHT ADAMS, WILD, SHACKLETON, PRIESTLEY ALBUMS (SPRI)

THE TORBAY HOTEL, TORQUAY, WHERE SHACKLETON HELD THE FAREWELL DINNER FOR THE *NIMROD* EXPEDITION IN AUGUST 1907   POST CODE: TQ2 5EY

Nimrod alongside in Torquay (SPRI)

After Shackleton was invalided home by Scott from the *Discovery* Expedition he was determined to lead his own expedition south. This expedition, called The British Antarctic Expedition, proved to be highly successful - a team led by Shackleton sledged to within 97 nautical miles of the South Pole, another team reached the South Magnetic Pole, a third climbed the active volcano Mount Erebus. The ship he used was a 136 foot Dundee-built whaling ship which he named *Nimrod*.

On the 30 July 1907 the *Nimrod* set sail for New Zealand from the East India Dock in London. Five days later King Edward VII and Queen Alexandra visited the ship at Cowes. However, the ship's final port of departure from Britain on 7 August 1907 was Torquay in South Devon.

*Nimrod under way leaving Torquay 7 August 1907
with the crew on deck waving goodbye   (SPRI)*

Why did Shackleton choose this small Devon seaside town to sail from, rather than, say, the more usual port of Plymouth? The naval port of Plymouth was the favoured port of departure for many explorers; and indeed Shackleton's *Endurance* and *Quest* left from there, following in the tradition set by Captain James Cook and others.

Torquay in August is a crowded place. It was as popular with Edwardian holidaymakers as it is today and it might have proved difficult to arrange the traditional farewell dinner for the officers and crew in a seafront hotel. However, this was done and it was held on the evening of 6 August in The Torbay Hotel. The Hotel still stands today and its façade and main function rooms are much as they were. The six-course menu shown overleaf offers some interesting dishes, named after the major backers of the expedition.

*The Torbay Hotel on the
Torquay sea front today
(Tim Burr)*

13

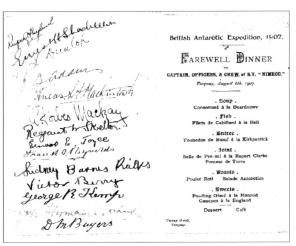

The menu from the Nimrod's Farewell Dinner, signed by the crew and VIPs (Athy Heritage Centre, Ireland)

The *Nimrod* did not revisit Torquay on its return in 1909. The Torquay museum has a letter to the Harbourmaster from Shackleton dated 27 August, thanking him for his courtesy, but stating he would not be coming alongside and because of his need to proceed at once back to London. Shackleton's wish quickly to proclaim the expedition's many achievements in the capital city obviously outweighed the need to pay another visit to the provincial seaside town.

But why did the Nimrod set sail from Torquay in the first place? At the time Ernest Shackleton had plenty on his mind and he did not leave with the *Nimrod*, which was skippered by Captain RG England. He was busy continuing to raise badly needed funds to pay for the expedition and also he felt the need to help his brother Frank with his financial problems and the suspicion that Frank had been implicated in the disappearance of the Irish crown jewels. And where was Frank at this time? He was spending the summer in a house in Torquay (called The Knoll) and Ernest's family, Emily and the children, were also staying in the town. It is therefore perhaps no surprise that the busy Shackleton chose to combine expedition and family matters and arranged for the *Nimrod* to depart from Torquay.

THE TERRA NOVA EXPEDITION

1910 - 13

'TERRA NOVA' VIEWED FROM AN ICE GROTTO BY HERBERT PONTING (SPRI)

OUTLANDS: THE DEVONPORT BIRTHPLACE OF CAPTAIN ROBERT FALCON SCOTT IN 1868

POSTCODE: PL2 3BZ

The Outlands plaque

On the old border of the towns of Plymouth and Devonport, close to the busy Milehouse road junction, is the site of Scott's birthplace, a large house called Outlands. Now it is the site of St Bartholomew's Church, a complex of modern flats and the Britannia Inn. The only part of Outlands which now remains is a section of the garden wall near the old main entrance on Scott Road. The house was hit by stray Luftwaffe bombs during the Plymouth blitz and for much of the 1950s it lay in ruins.

Outlands in 1894 from a water colour by Florence Murray

16

Robert Falcon Scott was born here on 6 June 1868. His grandfather had bought Outlands on his retirement from the Navy in the 1820s and his father, John Scott, lived here with his family while running the Hoegate Street Brewery on the Barbican. According to the 1871 census the family that lived here consisted of John and his wife Hannah, their four children, an aged aunt Charlotte and several servants. Although John Scott had a position in local society, serving as a Devonport magistrate and a churchwarden at St Mark's at Ford, the family were not affluent and struggled to make ends meet. Some have suggested that the last, dying written words of Scott, 'For God's sake look after our people', were in part influenced by the memory of difficulties of managing on limited finances.

The recollections of Scott's boyhood friends in the 1950s and those of his sisters suggest that Robert (or Con as he was known to the family) had a pleasant childhood playing and having adventures in the grounds of the house and, riding his pony 'Beppo' to the private day school at Exmouth House in the village of Stoke Damerel. Family stories recount that he was considered to have delicate health and was sick at the sight of blood. There are also accounts of him learning to sail with his father and brother in Plymouth Sound in an 18 foot boat with a big lug sail.

The newsletter of St. Bartholemew's Church, Outlands, from June 1968, the centenary of Scott's birth, showing a young Robert Scott.

At the age of 12, Con was sent away to Stubbington School near Fareham to be coached for his entry to Britannia Naval College at Dartmouth. At that time the College was based aboard two old hulks moored on the River Dart and life there was harsh.

Scott's naval career proved very successful and as an eighteen year old midshipman he greatly impressed Sir Clements Markham during a sailing contest in the Caribbean. Markham was looking for a young ambitious naval officer to command a British expedition to the Antarctic that he was beginning to plan and he placed Scott on his shortlist of contenders.

Scott returned to Devonport Naval Base for three years in 1891 to learn the new skills of torpedo warfare. This coincided with a financial crisis in his family which led to the family moving to Holcombe in Somerset and Outlands being rented out. Further financial difficulties followed the death of John Scott and then of Con's brother Archie. The young naval officer Robert Scott now had the burden of providing income for his mother and sisters.

In 1899 Scott applied for the post of commander of the National Antarctic (*Discovery*) Expedition organised under the leadership of Sir Clements Markham. Later, Scott's sister commented that Scott had no love of ice and snow but he had grown restless in the Navy and had now, of course, the need to provide financially for his mother and family. His application some have suggested may also have been prompted by his knowledge that his boyhood home was very close to Swilly House, now long gone, but located in the North Prospect housing estate. Swilly House was the birthplace of Tobias Furneaux who sailed with James Cook.

Commander of the *Adventure* during the voyage of 1772-75, Furneaux was very unlucky not to have been made famous for being the first man to view many of the islands on the fringe of the Antarctic continent. Though he passed within forty miles of South Georgia and Elephant Island he missed sighting them as they were at the time shrouded by a thick fog bank. Incidentally, Furneaux died in 1781 and is buried in Stoke Damerel churchyard.

It is recorded that Scott returned to Outlands on two occasions. Once when he was commanding HMS *Bulwark* and the ship visited Devonport in 1908, and he also returned to visit Outlands just before he left England to sail for the last time to Antarctica aboard *Terra Nova*. On that occasion, he carved 'SCOTT' on a birch tree he had long before planted in the grounds. After his death, the carving was preserved and mounted, and this is now on display in Plymouth City Museum on North Hill.

Preserved bark with Scott's carved name at Plymouth City Museum (Tim Burr)

The Plymouth bungalow in Peverell named 'Terra Nova': the home of Fred Parsons, Petty Officer on *Terra Nova*

POSTCODE: PL3 4PR

The former home of Petty Officer Fred Parsons on Churchill Way, Plymouth

In the 1950s and 60s the people of the City of Plymouth knew local businessman Fred Parsons for one thing…boot and shoe repairs. He had a very successful business on Hastings Street and a fleet of delivery vans that toured the City. He was a well known entrepreneur and famed for his slogans such as 'we will collect, repair and deliver within four hours'. The clue to his other claim to fame can be found at the bungalow he lived in for many years as it is called 'Terra Nova'. He lived in Plymouth until the age of 91 and was for many years the oldest survivor of Captain Scott's British Antarctic Expedition. In later life he wrote an account of his memories of his time aboard *Terra Nova*.

*Fred Parsons' boot and shoe repairing factory with delivery vans,
Hastings Street, Plymouth, in the 1950s (Jean Scholar)*

Fred Parsons volunteered to join Scott's Antarctic expedition
after seeing an article in the *Western Morning News*. He applied
with support of a senior submarine officer and was interviewed
by Captain Scott at the expedition HQ in London in April 1910.
The interview was brief and efficient, Scott appearing to put
great store on the personal recommendation of a fellow senior
officer. Parsons later recalled that Scott was physically on the
short side and how he was 'always courteous and a perfect
gentleman'.

As a crew member on the ship, Fred Parsons did not participate
in the expeditions on shore and so did not have experience of the
sledging journeys. Nevertheless, his recollections of the
expedition which he wrote in later life are of considerable
interest from his perspective as an ordinary member of the crew.

*Some of the crew of Terra Nova,
December 1910 (Fred Parsons far left)
by Herbert Ponting (SPRI)*

The British Antarctic Expedition was largely financed through private and commercial donations. It was decided to make Cardiff the home port of the *Terra Nova* due to the generosity of the local businessmen, particularly the Crown Patent Fuel Company which donated 300 tons of compressed coal briquettes. A farewell dinner was held on 13 June 1910 at the Royal Hotel for both officers and crew. Parsons recalls that, once the wealthy ship-owners were well oiled with whisky, they competed with each other with their donations. The event was undoubtedly boisterous and one guest was said to have got up on the long table and marched up and down saying, 'I'll give £500 if my brother will do the same'.

The ship stopped briefly on its voyage south at Madeira to take on supplies. Relations between the crew and one of the scientists were clearly developing well. Parsons recalls being taken by the scientists, to lunch in a first class hotel on the island and being encouraged to relax in what he regarded as 'posh surroundings'.

The final port of departure before setting out for Antarctica was Port Lyttelton in New Zealand. Here all the expedition equipment on the ship was unloaded and then it was checked on shore. The crew was turned out of its quarters under the forecastle to make space for ten of the 19 Manchurian ponies which were to be transported to Antarctica to provide haulage for the explorers. The ponies were slung on board using masthead and yard-arm tackles and, once there, they were boxed in for the duration of the month's journey south. One of the many discomforts the crew had to bear was that their new quarters were under the stables for the ponies on the deck and there was no protection for the men from the animals' mess which regularly flowed through from above. Fred Parsons recalled that one of his particular jobs during these preparations was to assist Edgar Evans in fitting the sledges with straps and rigging using the skills of boot-making, a skill he had learnt from his grandfather.

The *Terra Nova* was very heavily laden and supplies were piled on the upper deck. Second in command Lieutenant Teddy Evans described the ship as like a floating farmyard with not an inch of deck space visible. On the poop deck the hayrick for ponies' feed was as high as the funnel. The three motor sledges (or tractors), thirty tons of coal and two and a half tons of petrol and paraffin were stowed on deck. It was completely overloaded. The Plimsoll line regulations were ignored. The ship sailed on 29 November 1910 and it was hit by a severe gale three days out. It reached force 10 and blew for three days. Working the sails proved very difficult as the deck was so full of cargo. Mountainous seas crashed over the sides and some supplies were lost. Dogs were in danger of being strangled by their leads and the ponies were badly knocked about. The seams on the deck opened up and water poured in below. Day and night the crew, officers and scientists worked the pumps to save the ship. They even had to resort to a bucket chain. Parsons had great admiration for the way the scientists, many of whom had no knowledge or experience of sailing, were prepared to climb aloft on violently swaying masts in sub-zero temperatures to help work the sails.

(SPRI)

Furling the main sail on Terra Nova in pack ice by Herbert Ponting

Scott's objective was to land close to his previous *Discovery* base in McMurdo Sound. They arrived on 4 January 1911 and crew, officers and scientists immediately set about unloading the ship and erecting the hut for the shore party. At one point a number of killer whales swam up, attracted by the ponies and dogs on the ice. Parsons was making fast the foresail, well out on the lower yard, and so had a good view of their arrival. He described how the whales gathered together under the ice and then came up as one in order to crack it in the hope that 'a meal of ponies and dogs would fall into their jaws'. Everything was quickly loaded back on board until the danger passed.

During the unloading one of the motor tractors fell through the ice and sank. Parsons' personal view was that this was not a particular concern to Captain Scott who saw them as mainly experimental.

Once the ship was unloaded and the main shore party settled, the next job of the crew was to take a party of six men to King Edward's Land to the east of the Great Ice Barrier. It was led by Lieutenant Campbell and included Petty Officer Frank Browning RN (who also came from Devon). The *Terra Nova* was sailing along the Ross Ice Shelf looking for a suitable landing place when the crew received a huge shock. There in this icy wasteland, just when the crew of the *Terra Nova* thought they were completely isolated from the rest of the world, was another vessel. It was Amundsen's ship, the *Fram*.

Amundsen, the Norwegian explorer, had announced to the world that he was taking the *Fram* north in 1910 to explore the Arctic. Once he learnt that two Americans had claimed that they had reached the North Pole he had changed his plan and turned south. Whilst docked in Melbourne, Australia, Scott had received a terse personal telegram from him which said he was headed south but Amundsen's precise plans were unclear and it was a real surprise to find him so close to Scott's base.

The *Terra Nova* made fast to the ice and contact was made with the Norwegians. Fred Parsons was very impressed by the way the dog drivers controlled their sledge teams. He described how he saw a dog team leave the *Fram* and move quickly across the ice. The team stopped alongside the *Terra Nova* in perfect order; the driver turned over his sledge and the dogs lay down, heads on their paws. Obviously, quite a contrast to the way the dogs of the British Antarctic Expedition were behaving.

Amundsen was welcomed aboard *Terra Nova* and a reciprocal visit was paid to *Fram*. Fred was impressed by the ship, noting that in contrast to *Terra Nova*, *Fram* had been specifically built for polar exploration. Clearly the visits were amicable and the crews cheered each other when the British ship sailed back to McMurdo Sound to relay the news of their discovery to Scott. Parsons simply records that when Scott received the reports on Amundsen 'it shook him up a bit'.

Fram in the foreground with Terra Nova behind 4 February 1911 (Sphere Magazine)

The *Terra Nova,* with Parsons and its crew, now returned to New Zealand for a planned refit during the winter. It returned to McMurdo Sound to re-supply Scott's base in January 1912 and then finally to collect the shore party in January 1913. They knew that Amundsen had beaten Scott to the Pole from the news they had received whilst waiting in New Zealand, but knew nothing of the tragedy that had overtaken Scott and the polar party during its return. The *Terra Nova* crew prepared a celebratory welcome on board ship for the men who had endured the hardships of two winters in the hostile environment of the Antarctic. The ship was scrubbed, ropes neatly coiled and flags hoisted aloft. A special meal with champagne was prepared and the mess room decked with little flags and silk ribbons. When the ship was within hailing distance, the crew learnt the news of the death of the polar party the previous year. Parsons recalled that 'the news took us aback and for some time we were unable to speak'. The flags were taken down and the mess room stripped. The crew's reaction was to get everything packed up as quickly as possible and get out.

Throughout the remainder of his life Fred Parsons spoke proudly of his service aboard *Terra Nova* and spoke highly of Captain Scott as a leader and a gentleman. It was only towards the end of

his life that there was some local interest in his exploits in Antarctica. He was a guest of honour at the opening of the film 'Scott of the Antarctic' at the Plymouth Odeon which was attended by the star, John Mills, in February 1949. When Plymouth celebrated the centenary of Scott's birth in 1968, Fred was invited to attend a number of the events including the unveiling of a statue to the explorer in St Mark's Church, Ford, and the opening of a display in the Civic Centre commemorating Scott's life.

Fred Parsons' skis, now made into a coat stand (Jean Scholar)

THE PLYMPTON MAN, FRANCIS DAVIES: THE SKILLED *TERRA NOVA* SHIPWRIGHT

Francis Davies with one of the seven mules which were brought to the shore base when the Terra Nova returned to the Antarctic in February 1913   (Joy Watts)

Francis Davies was a Plymothian who lived at Nicholls Farm, Plympton and later at Saltram Villas, Laira PL3 6AQ. He was recruited to serve on *Terra Nova* as Leading Shipwright and was responsible for two notable tasks during the expedition. He was responsible for the erection of the huts at Cape Evans and the construction of the memorial cross, which was placed on Observation Point overlooking McMurdo Sound, to commemorate Scott and the polar party. He also was witness, as was fellow Plymothian Petty Officer Fred Parsons, to the extraordinary meeting of *Terra Nova* with Amunsden's ship *Fram* in the Bay of Whales. All these events are written up in his account of his experiences called 'With Scott: Before the Mast', written under the pseudonym Rudolf.

Nicholls Farm, Plympton today.
(John Boulden)

27

Francis Davies was a very experienced carpenter and shipwright and was responsible for several modifications to *Terra Nova* before it sailed. As the ship's chippy, it fell to Davies to be responsible for the hut which was used as living quarters for the 19 officers and 14 men of the shore party. A trial erection was made alongside the quay in Lyttelton, New Zealand, which was a wise precaution as it was imperative that the huts were constructed quickly not knowing what the weather would be on arrival in McMurdo Sound.

Once the huts and essential stores were unloaded work started. The main timbers were prepared and cut to size in advance. The floor area was 50 feet by 25 feet and vertical tongue and groove matchboard was nailed both inside and outside the framework to form an air space. A layer of sea grass sewn into jute sacking was given a further covering of weather boarding inside and out. Similar construction was used for the roof and floor with the addition of a layer of 'rubberoid'. The door opened into an airtight porch. Everything was done to make the structure windproof. There were three small double paned (non opening) windows. During the construction geologists' hammers were pressed into use as were their spiked boots for roof work. Black volcanic ash and forage bales were piled up along the outside walls for further protection from the elements. Inside, Scott had a bulkhead of packing cases arranged to divide the officers' from the men's quarters. However, unlike Shackleton, he shared his corner cubicle with Lt Teddy Evans and Dr Edward Wilson. Victor Campbell reported that Davies worked for 48 hours without a break to finish the job and the shore party were delighted to take up residence in their new living quarters. Scott wrote '…we are simply overwhelmed by its comfort'.

Francis Davies fixing insulation to the hut wall at Cape Evans
by Herbert Ponting (SPRI)

Francis Davies was enlisted as a member of the ship's party so he returned to New Zealand with *Terra Nova* once the shore party was settled. He returned with the ship to re-supply the shore base in January 1913, carrying onboard a number of mules which were to be used for haulage. Davies recorded in his account that on their arrival 'Commander Evans hailed the shore party, asking if all was well. Lieutenant Campbell replied, and informed us that Captain Scott and his party had reached the Pole on 17th January (1911) and all had perished on the return journey from exposure and want…- there was a deadly silence, broken only by the noise of the skua gulls'.

Before departing it was decided to place a permanent memorial to the dead, and Davies was given the job of constructing the nine foot high cross. He chose to use the extremely hard Australian jarra wood and it was painted white.

Apsley Cherry-Garrard, the young assistant zoologist, chose the words from Tennyson's poem Ulysses: 'To strive, to seek, to find and not to yield' which were engraved on to the cross along with the names of the five who perished. It proved a difficult task to drag the cross to the 750 foot high summit and erect it, and it took the men two days.

After a short service led by surgeon Edward Atkinson, who had now assumed command of the expedition, the men left the Antarctic and the cross on Observation Hill behind, where it still stands today, facing south to the Pole.

The Memorial Cross built by Davies still stands proud on Observation Hill (The Sphere 24 May 1913)

For many years the Royal Yacht Squadron White Ensign from *Terra Nova* was displayed in the Plympton St Maurice Masonic Lodge. This flag, mounted in a purpose built oak frame, was presented to the Lodge by (Brother) Francis Davies. It was auctioned at Christie's in 1999 with an estimate of £7,000.

THE PLAQUE IN TORQUAY TOWN HALL TO A 'GALLANT' ANTARCTIC HERO: FRANK BROWNING, PETTY OFFICER ON *TERRA NOVA*

POSTCODE: TQ1 3DR

Plaque in Torquay Town Hall (Tim Burr)

In the foyer of Torquay Town Hall stands this large plaque to Frank Browning. Who was he and what was the nature of his 'Gallant work in Antarctic Exploration'?

The *Torquay Times* of March 1930 announced that the Torquay Citizens' League Committee had launched a public appeal for funds for a commemorative tablet to Frank Browning following his death. He had died at the relatively young age of 48. He was well known in the Torquay area then, but is somewhat forgotten now.

Petty Officer Frank Browning (Torquay Museum)

31

In 1910 Petty Officer Browning was recruited by Captain Scott to join the shore party of the *Terra Nova* Antarctic expedition. He was one of six men who became the Northern Expeditionary Party. This group suffered enormous physical and mental hardship as they were forced to winter for six months, unprepared, in an ice cave when they were marooned on the shore of the Ross Sea. The story of the ordeal of these six men is one of the great stories of suffering and heroic survival; and this Torquay man was an important part of it.

Members of the Northern Party. Front row: Priestley, Campbell and Murray Levick (operating the camera shutter by a string). Back row: Abbott, Dickason and Browning   (SPRI)

A primary aim of Scott's *Terra Nova* expedition was scientific research, continuing the work he had begun on the *Discovery* Expedition. Scott therefore sent small exploring expeditions out from the base at Cape Evans in several directions. The scientists in the Northern Party were geologist Raymond Priestley and surgeon and zoologist Murray Levick. After collecting samples and making scientific observations for nearly a year, and living in a hut at Cape Adare, they moved to a place they called Inexpressible Island to carry on their work, expecting to be picked up by *Terra Nova* in February 1912. The ship failed to arrive because of the heavy pack ice. With the harsh Antarctic winter setting in they had no option but to sit it out and wait for better weather. The men hollowed out an underground ice cave and lived a squalid, cramped existence for months on end. Weak with starvation and dysentery, they then faced a 230 mile gruelling journey, over land and across pack ice, back to the base hut. Here, on their arrival in November 1912, they learnt the news of Captain Scott's death. This event was so dramatic and terrible that for years it overshadowed the story of the men of the Northern Party.

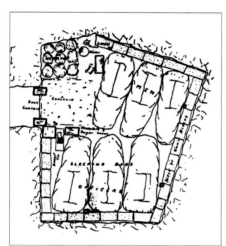

Plan of the ice cave showing the position of the men's and officers' sleeping bags. Campbell helped relations by drawing an imaginary line between the two rows of bags and encouraging everyone to treat it as a soundproof wall. (Priestley 'Antarctic Adventure' Fisher Unwin 1914)

Campbell's drawing of the interior of the ice cave. Priestley sits in his bag, Dickason cooks   (SPRI)

Conditions in the 12 foot by 9 foot ice cave were terrible. It was impossible to stand up fully as it was about five and a half feet in height. They rarely went out. For entertainment, they read aloud from Boccaccio's *Decameron* and Dickens *Great Expectations*. On Sundays they sang hymns and read from the Bible. Food consisted of seal meat and blubber warmed on a blubber stove and supplemented by the occasional treat of a handful of raisins. Sledging rations had to be saved for the eventual trek back to the base hut. Browning suffered with chronic diarrhoea and his mouth was covered with sores but as Priestley later wrote Browning was unfailingly cheerful and '...he had a fund of anecdote and repartee, and was never at a loss for a good answer.' It was said that his tales of his boyhood life on a Devonshire farm at Stockland kept his comrades amused for hours. Although seriously ill on the trek back to the Cape Evans base, and being carried part way on the sledge, he insisted on walking the final stage of the journey so it could be said all the men returned on foot. On their return to the base many were surprised at how relaxed and easy the relationship was between the men and how there was no sign of division. This seems all the more remarkable, given their deprivation. Browning was an inspiration and was a true gallant hero.

On his return from the Antarctic Frank Browning married Marjorie Bending and they lived on Windsor Road, Ellacombe, in Torquay. They had two children Mary and Peter.

Emerging from the ice cave after six months imprisonment covered in grease and smoke from the blubber stove- Priestley, Murray Levick and Browning (SPRI)

G Murray Levick: Terra Nova surgeon who retired to Budleigh Salterton

POST CODE EX9 7AP

Murray Levick served as naval surgeon and zoologist aboard *Terra Nova* and was an important member of the unlucky six-man Northern Expedition (which included Frank Browning). He retired to Budleigh Salterton and became a well known character in this small Devon seaside town. He died there in May 1956 at the age of 79.

Murray Levick's house at Ting Tong, Budleigh Salterton

After qualifying as a doctor from St Batholemew's Hospital, Murray Levick joined the Royal Navy specialising in methods of maintaining physical fitness. He served on HMS *Essex,* commanded by Captain Scott, and in 1910 he joined the *Terra Nova* expedition. Levick turned out to be not the liveliest member of the ward room and came in for a fair amount of teasing. His nickname was The Old Sport or Mother. 'Rubicund of countenance and renowned in the world of sport, slow to move and act, but wise at bottom, he had a magnificent fund of anecdote...His habits were secretive. Like a jackdaw he acquired articles and hid them, and then forgot all about them...'wrote fellow naval surgeon, Edward Atkinson.

Murray Levick (in his rabbit hat) pouring whisky down the throat of a pony, who had swam ashore from the ship, in a desperate attempt to warm up the animal. It later died from the experience.
8 February 1911 by Herbert Ponting (SPRI)

As a member of the Northern Party Levick's duties were to be photographer, medical officer and to be in charge of stores as well as carry out scientific work. The party's first base was at Cape Adare, located in the middle of a stinking penguin rookery, where Levick made a meticulous study of penguin behaviour. His groundbreaking book was published in 1914 and it remained a standard work for many years.

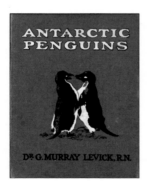

Murray Levick proved to be stoic in the face of the ordeal of surviving in the ice cave at Inexpressible Island and in his blubber-stained diary (now in the archive at the SPRI) he recorded many fascinating insights into the mental and physical condition of the men. He took it upon himself to defuse arguments where he could and was most caring towards the members of the party who fell ill, especially Frank Browning. The major call for his skills as a surgeon came when Abbott cut three of his fingers of his hand to the bone whilst killing a seal. Levick wrote: 'My hands were filthy and soaked in blubber from the stove, and my fingers stiff with cold, besides which we only had the guttering light of a blubber lamp.' Despite the conditions, Levick's care in dressing the wounds meant gangrene was avoided. It is recorded that he also proved inventive in using items in the medicine bag to enliven their tedious diet making good use of bottles of ginger, lime juice and citron tablets!

This experience of survival in the ice cave was put to use during the Second World War when Levick gave advice to a plan, hatched by British Intelligence, to seal six men up inside the Rock of Gibraltar once it had fallen to the Germans. Code named TRACER, the plan was to seal the men up inside a 45 foot long cave for the duration of the occupation and provide them with a radio so they could send out messages about enemy movements. Levick provided advice about all aspects of survival in a confined space, including suitable clothing, exercise, sanitation and how to dispose of any member of the team who died. The plan was never put into operation as German attention turned away from Gibraltar; but a survival manual was produced for similar operations in future wars.

In later life Murray Levick devoted much of his time to organising expeditions for the British Schools' Exploring Society which he founded in 1932. He led annual expeditions to places such as Finland, Lapland and Newfoundland and remained the Society's President for the rest of his life. The little Devon seaside town of Budleigh Salterton, with its connections with Sir Walter Raleigh, proved a fitting retirement home for this many-faceted man of the sea.

THE MODEL OF *TERRA NOVA* IN PLYMOUTH CITY MUSEUM MADE BY PETTY OFFICER PATRICK KEOHANE, WHO RETIRED TO PLYMOUTH

POSTCODE: PL4 8AJ

Plymouth City Museum on North Hill has a small but fascinating collection of artefacts relating to the heroic age of Antarctic exploration. One of their prized displays is of this model of Scott's ship the *Terra Nova* made by Petty Officer Patrick Keohane. It was made during the long dark winter days in the expedition hut. The model is highly detailed and complete with sails, ropes and blocks. The Museum also has a set of skis donated by Keohane in 1945. These skis were originally Captain Scott's; he having given them to Keohane, it is said, as they fitted the Petty Officer better.

Patrick Keohane constructing a model of the Terra Nova in the expedition hut by Herbert Ponting

(SPRI)

Keohane was the eldest of ten children in a family from Coolbawn in Ireland. He joined the Navy at sixteen and trained on HMS *Impregnable*, operating from Plymouth. He served with Scott's second in command for the Antarctic expedition, Teddy Evans, and at interview with Scott for a position on the expedition Keohane is said to have answered the question, 'Why do you want to go?' by saying: 'I always want to see what's on the other side of the hill!'

Keohane proved to be a tough, resilient and reliable man and was regularly chosen for sledging trips. He was an important part of one of the support teams for the Southern Party, led by Scott, which was aiming to reach the South Pole. Keohane was in a team with Cherry-Garrard, Bowers and fellow Irishman Crean for the gruelling 125 mile slog up the Beardmore Glacier when they advanced as little as 4 miles a day. He suffered very badly with snow blindness and was described by Bowers as being: 'blind as a bat'. On 21 December 1911, with 350 miles to go to the Pole, Keohane was selected, with three others, to return. He was, therefore, one of the last to see the Polar Party alive as they headed further south over the polar plateau. No one knew that Amundsen had already reached the Pole a week before.

Hauling an 800lb sledge up the crevassed Beardmore Glacier, December 1911. Keohane is third from left *(SPRI)*

Keohane was also part of the team led by the newly promoted commander of the expedition, Edward Atkinson, who, in November 1912, searched for Scott and his four companions when they failed to return from the Pole. When the frozen bodies were found in the final camp, just 11 nautical miles from the One Ton Camp supply dump, the tent was collapsed over them with a cairn and cross built over it.

Extract from Patrick Keohane's diary 12 November 1912

'We plodded on through the soft snow. Close to the end of our march we sighted what we thought was one of last year's cairns …on approaching it, Mr Wright found it to be a tent covered in a winter's snow…So we directed our course towards it with heavy hearts, for here we knew at least that some of our comrades lay sleeping.

After digging for some time, we uncovered the tent. We found only three of them in it so we knew that trouble must have started early on the return march. We found the bodies of Captain Scott, Dr Wilson and Lieutenant Bowers. …We found three pairs of skis, all lying down as they were taken off. Three harnesses were attached to the sledge so all three men were pulling but the poor fellows were in a terrible state.

The party arrived here on 21 March and camped, hoping to go on to One Ton (camp) the next morning. But when they awoke, it was a howling blizzard and continued until the 29th, which was the last entry in the diary. They had only two cups of tea since the 21st.'

The inner tent in which Scott and his two companions were discovered. Once the bodies had been identified, and personal possessions removed, the tent was lowered and a large cairn of snow was erected over them. They remain there still. (The Sphere 24 May 1913)

Some of the shore party in 1911, photographed by Herbert Ponting,
outside the hut at Cape Evans. Standing from left: Nelson, Teddy Evans,
Oates, Atkinson, Scott, Wright, Keohane, Gran and Lashly.   *(SPRI)*
Sitting from left: Meares, Debenham, Wilson, Simpson and Edgar Evans

During the First World War, Patrick Keohane spent three years
in Plymouth as a training officer back on HMS *Impregnable*. He
then saw active service aboard the cruiser *Cornwall*. Between
the wars, he joined the coastguard service stationed in Ireland
and the Isle of Man. After serving in the Second World War,
Keohane retired, with his wife and daughter (who was named
Nova, after *Terra Nova*), to Plymouth, his original base port. His
retirement home was 1, Birchfield Avenue in Beacon Park, PL2
3LA. It is said he enjoyed his retirement, sailing frequently in
Plymouth Sound, and living until the age of 71.

THE NATIONAL MEMORIAL TO CAPTAIN SCOTT AND THE POLAR PARTY, MOUNT WISE, DEVONPORT

POSTCODE: PL1 4JQ

*The Scott Memorial
at Mount Wise,
Devonport
(Tim Burr)*

When the news of Captain Scott's death reached England in February 1913 there was an outpouring of public grief, similar it is said to that which occurred at the news of the death of Diana, Princess of Wales. In response to this a Mansion House Scott Memorial Fund was established which was launched by the Lord Mayor of London.

This fund was designed to support the families of the dead explorers and to construct fitting permanent memorials. When the Fund closed the resources available exceeded expectations and there was sufficient remaining to establish the Scott Polar Research Institute at the University of Cambridge. This notion was first discussed amongst the scientists before they returned from the Antarctic and a leading advocate was the young geologist Frank Debenham, who became the Institute's first Director in 1920.

The funds made available for memorials provided for one in St. Paul's Cathedral and a National Memorial for all the five explorers who died. Several ideas and designs for the National Memorial were submitted, including one from the *Sphere* magazine which proposed a London monument in Waterloo Place showing just three of the dead and with penguins standing guard.

The Sphere Magazine proposal for a London memorial to Captain Scott and his companions, 24 May 1913

The organising committee chose a design called 'Pro Patria' by the Glasgow School of Art trained sculpture Albert Hodge. Hodge proposed an allegorical group in bronze on a granite base. In the original design, the group was to represent Courage

43

sustained by Patriotism, spurning Fear, Despair and Death, with the figure of Courage being crowned by Immortality. Following complaints from some fellows of the Royal Geographical Society and Kathleen Scott, Hodge made substantial revisions to his design. The figures representing Fear, Despair and Death were removed and the main figure was given a more contemplative pose and sledging gear in a direct representation of Captain Scott. Hodge's inclusion of a pair of snow shoes was altered to a pair of skis when Cherry Garrard pointed out the error, as snow shoes were not used during the expedition. The four bronze panels on the podium depict the words from Tennyson, 'To strive; to seek; to find and not to yield', and show bronze portrait medallions of the five men.

The initial plan was to site this monument in London but all the proposed locations, including beside the National Portrait Gallery, Victoria Tower Gardens and Greenwich Hospital, met difficulties. This all caused delay which was compounded by the death of Hodge in 1917. In the end the site at Mount Wise in Devonport was chosen and the National Memorial for the victims of the expedition was unveiled on 10 August 1925. The final cost of the Mount Wise memorial was £12,000 and it was unveiled by Commodore Charles Royds, who had been an officer on the *Discovery* Expedition. Captain Scott's son, Peter, attended the ceremony and laid a wreath. By the time of the eventual unveiling about thirty other memorials in Britain alone had been erected, including the one in Exeter Cathedral and one at the Royal Britannia Naval College in Dartmouth.

Pamphlet issued by The Lord Mayor's Fund (Seamus Taaffe)

Captain Charles Royds unveiling the Memorial 10 August 1925
(Doidge's Annual 1926)

15 year old Peter Scott
laying a wreath
(Doidge's Annual 1926)

Around the base of the memorial, and set in the ground, is an extract from Captain Scott's closing passage in his Message to the Public, written as he and his comrades were dying in their tent:

We took risks, we knew we took them; things have come out against us, and therefore we have no cause for complaint, but bow to the will of Providence,...

Had we lived, I should have had a tale to tell of the hardihood, endurance, and courage of my companions which would have stirred the heart of every Englishman. These rough notes and our dead bodies must tell the tale.

THE PLYMOUTH ODEON CINEMA, NEW GEORGE STREET: LOCATION OF THE COMMAND PERFORMANCE OF THE FILM 'SCOTT OF THE ANTARCTIC'

Film star John Mills meets some of the survivors of Scott's Antarctic Expeditions at the first screening of the film 'Scott of the Antarctic' at the Plymouth Odeon, 22 Feb 1949. L to R: Fred Parsons (Terra Nova), John Mills, penguin, Fred Dailey (Discovery), Patrick Keohane (Terra Nova), Miss Palmer and the niece of Edgar Evans (Terra Nova). (Jean Scholar)

Produced by Michael Balcon and directed by Charles Frend, the film was an instant box office success. It was filmed in Norway, Switzerland and at Ealing Studios and sought to faithfully recount the story. Several former members of the expedition, such as Frank Debenham and Raymond Priestley, acted as advisers and some of the original equipment was used, including Wilson's medical chest and the horn gramophone taken to the Cape Evans hut.

The Director did admit to altering the story of the occasion when Scott heard the news of Amundsen's decision to head for the South Pole in order to avoid confusion in the film goer's mind.

Great care was made to secure authenticity in the film; even to the extent of reconstructing some of the classic images taken in the expedition hut (David James, Scott of the Antarctic, Convoy publications 1948)

The Command Performance of the film in Plymouth was quite an occasion. The great and the good were invited as well as some survivors of the expedition. The *Western Morning News* of 22 February 1949 reported that police had to keep back excited crowds outside the Plymouth Odeon when John Mills, the actor who played the part of Captain Scott, made a personal appearance before the showing of the film.

'I have never had such a wonderful reception,' he said, adding: 'The crowd was not hysterical nor did they try to tear my hat off, as sometimes has been the case.'

Former Terra Nova Petty Officer Fred Parsons with polar display at the Odeon Cinema on the occasion of the first screening of the film 'Scott of the Antarctic' in Plymouth. The exhibition shows Fred Parsons' skis (made into a coat stand), a penguin caught and stuffed by him and the model of the Terra Nova made by Patrick Keohane. (*Peter Warren*)

The Odeon Cinema on New George Street was demolished in June 1963. The Plymouth Littlewoods department store now occupies on the site.

MEMENTOES AND MEMORIALS: REMEMBERING CAPTAIN SCOTT

The death of Captain Scott became an occasion for national mourning. A memorial service was held in St Paul's Cathedral on 14 February 1913 which was attended by King George V- an unprecedented act. The monarch had never before attended a service for someone not a member of the Royal Family. An immense crowd of people came to watch the service which in itself was a strange event, without bodies to be the focus of the grief. Similar services were held all around the country and many places erected some form of memorial. In addition, much commemorative memorabilia was produced.

Some of the mementoes produced after Scott's death including a tin tea caddy, music hall song, china figure, postcards and books (Tim Burr)

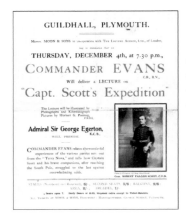

Commander Teddy Evans fulfilled Scott's commitments to the prearranged speaking tour which had been an essential part of the fund-raising for the expedition. He spoke at 50 venues from 13 October to 20 December 1913 across the country from Edinburgh to Brighton, coming to Plymouth on 4 December.

The plaque to the Polar Party in the Chapel at The Royal Naval College, Dartmouth TQ6 0HJ, which Scott attended when it was housed in two hulks moored on the River Dart in South Devon.

The City of Plymouth has remembered its famous Antarctic hero in a number of ways over the years. For instance, in 1956 Peter Scott reopened the Plymouth Central Library after its reconstruction following the bombing of April 1941. The new Lecture Theatre was named the Scott Theatre after his father. The most notable commemorations in the City were in 1968 on the centenary of his birth. Events were organised for a couple of days around 6 June; many attended by some survivors of the *Terra Nova* Expedition, including Sir Raymond Priestley.

First Day Cover from Scott's Centenary in 1968, franked with the special Plymouth postmark, showing his birthplace Outlands

In the 1930s, when the City Council built new houses on the land around Scott's birthplace at Outlands PL2 3BZ, the streets were named after each member of the final Polar Party on the Terra Nova Expedition. The small area adjacent to the roads, where the garages were located, was named Evans Place, after Petty Officer Evans.

This bust of Captain Scott by his wife Kathleen was presented to Devonport Council after his death. Now it is located within Stoke Damerel Community College PL3 4BD, the school nearest his birthplace.

The rededication of the National Scott Memorial at Mount Wise 23rd March 2012 attended by HRH The Princess Royal.

Captain Scott's grandchildren at the Scott Memorial, Dafila Scott, Falcon Scott and Nicola Starks.

THE ENDURANCE EXPEDITION

1914 - 17

'ENDURANCE' CRUSHED BY THE ICE
BY FRANK HURLEY (SPRI)

ENDURANCE LEAVES PLYMOUTH IN AUGUST 1914

August 1914 was a turbulent time in Britain for we were on the brink of war with Germany. *Endurance* left its South West India London dock on 1 August, the day Germany declared war on Russia. On 4 August the ship was moored in Great Western Docks (now called Millbay Dock), Plymouth PL1 3EW when the order for a general mobilisation of troops in Britain was given. After consulting the crew Sir Ernest Shackleton boldly declared that the ship and its men were at the disposal of the Government, writing that 'there were enough trained and experienced men among us to man a destroyer.' After so much planning for this ambitious expedition Shackleton must have felt very nervous of the Admiralty's reply. When the answer came it was in the form of a one word telegram from Whitehall. It simply said: 'Proceed'. Later the First Lord of the Admiralty, Winston Churchill, sent a longer cable saying the Government wished for the expedition to take place as planned. On 8 August *Endurance* left Plymouth to sail to the Weddell Sea in Antarctica by way of South America and South Georgia.
She was not to return.

ENDURANCE LEAVES PLYMOUTH.

VOYAGE TO BUENOS AYRES BEGUN.

The Endurance, one of the two vessels to be used by Sir Ernest Shackleton in his forthcoming Antarctic expedition, left Plymouth on Saturday for Buenos Ayres. During her stay at Plymouth the Endurance has been moored at the pontoon in the Great Western Docks, and yesterday at noon, after making a detour of the Sound, she entered on her long voyage to South America, which it is expected will last about 40 days. The Endurance is under the command of Lieut. Worsey, R.N.R.

Sir Ernest Shackleton arrived at Plymouth on Friday to see the ship off, and he was on board as she passed through the Sound. He then came ashore in a pinnace. On account of the adverse weather the vessel's departure was not witnessed by many people.

The personnel of the Endurance includes an old Plymouth and Mannamead College boy, Dr. A. H. Macklin.

Western Morning News 10 August 1914

54

Local press reports of the departure mention the poor weather for August. This is confirmed in the diary of Thomas Orde Lees, motor expert and later storekeeper for the expedition. The diary is now archived at the Scott Polar Research Institute in Cambridge MS 1652 BJ. His entry for 8 August 1914 reads:

Very worst West country weather, blowing hard and drizzling rain. The ship was alongside Millbay wharf when we went on board and she left there sharp noon today with Sir Ernest on board. Just a very small crowd to see us off, but enthusiastic enough... Sir Ernest slept at the Duke of Cornwall's Hotel, he offered me a bed very kindly but declined as I thought it best to get into the routine as quickly as possible. Before we got outside the breakwater, Sir Ernest left the ship in a picket boat lent to him by the C in C.

The imposing Duke of Cornwall Hotel where Shackleton stayed before the departure of the Endurance from Millbay Dock

The Duke of Cornwall Hotel was built in 1863 to serve the needs of the South Devon Railway (which had its Plymouth Millbay station on the current site of Plymouth Pavilions) and to link with the Atlantic liners which berthed at the nearby dock. This grand hotel was the obvious choice for Sir Ernest Shackleton and it would have been the natural venue for a final dinner before departure (although no record of such an event has yet been found).

The dining room of the Duke of Cornwall Hotel (Jonathan Morcom)

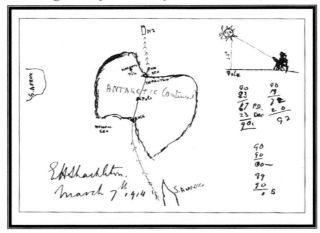

Shackleton's sketch of his proposed route across the Antarctic Continent drawn on the back of a menu card at a fund raising dinner held in London by the Devonian Association on 7 March 1914.

Shackleton's plan was to arrange for a second ship, the *Aurora,* to take a party of men to the Ross Sea side of the continent and for them to lay supply depots along the route to the South Pole. These depots would then be used by Shackleton and his men crossing from the Weddell Sea. Despite a terrible ordeal, which included the loss of three of their number, these men of the Ross Sea Party managed carry out their task. One local connection with this part of the expedition is Devonport seaman William Mugridge who was a stoker on *Aurora* and who lived on James Street.

R S CLARK: MARINE BIOLOGIST AT THE PLYMOUTH MARINE BIOLOGICAL ASSOCIATION AND SURVIVOR OF THE ORDEAL ON ELEPHANT ISLAND

POSTCODE: PL1 2PB

Robert Selbie Clark was born in Scotland and whilst working at the Edinburgh Scottish Oceanographical Laboratory began studying in Antarctic marine life, working under Dr W.S. Bruce the leader of the *Scotia* Expedition (1902 to 1904). He was appointed as naturalist at the Plymouth Marine Biological Association (MBA) in 1913 and the following year he joined Ernest Shackleton's *Endurance* expedition. In doing so he was following in the footsteps of other MBA scientists who had served on Antarctic expeditions, namely T.V. Hodgson on *Discovery* and Edward Nelson on *Terra Nova*

RS Clark working, with his microscope, on Endurance by Frank Hurley (SPRI)

When in the ice of the Weddell Sea, Clark successfully hauled up a wide variety of marine specimens using dredges at several hundreds of fathoms. This was tough and heavy work as the mud froze when it was hauled to the surface. On one occasion Shackleton wrote that one day... 'We heard a great yell from the (ice) floe and found Clark dancing about and shouting Scottish war-cries. He had secured his first complete specimen of Antarctic fish, apparently a new species'.

Thomas Orde Lees in his diary wrote that Clark was ... 'A typical Scotsman - but a thoroughly good sort. He is a footballer of some merit. He is very hardworking, forever skinning penguins,..(and)...Clark has become quite an expert taxidermist,…I made a good bargain with him some time ago, giving Clark a pair of leather mitts for a dressed Emperor's skin. The next day new leather mitts were served out. Clark got the "hump"!'

The three open boats which saved the crew of the sunken Endurance pulled up on Elephant Island by Frank Hurley 15 April 1916   (SPRI)

When *Endurance* was crushed by the ice and sank, Clark's marine specimens were lost. This must have been a severe blow for this dedicated scientist. The main purpose for his involvement in the expedition had gone. Clark had to endure the fearful seven day open boat journey across the freezing Southern Ocean to Elephant Island. The men then had to somehow survive for four winter months under two of the upturned boats in the bitter wind while Shackleton went for help. Clark chose to sleep in the thwarts of the upturned boats on two rudders. The great discomfort of sleeping 'upstairs' (as it was called) was that there was insufficient headroom to sit up and these men had to have their meals leaning half up on their elbows.

Despite the appalling conditions on this bleak island, Clark did manage to carry on with some scientific work. He recorded the contents of the stomachs of the 1,400 Gentoo penguins which were killed for food and fuel. He noted that the quantity of the crustacean *Euphausia* was enormous for the size of bird. Such was his dedication to science that Shackleton included an appendix written by RS Clark in his famous book 'South' published in 1919. It was entitled 'South Atlantic Whales and Whaling' and drew on his study during the voyage to the Antarctic and his time on South Georgia.

Described by Frank Hurley, the photographer, 'As the most motley and unkempt assembly that was ever projected on to plate' R S Clark is fourth from the right on the back row in a big dark balaclava, with not such a happy face! 10 May 1916 Elephant Island (SPRI)

On his return to Britain R S Clark, like many of the men, enlisted and went to war, serving on a mine sweeper. He then returned to his post in Plymouth before becoming an eminent researcher into the fishing industry as Director of the Scottish Home Office Marine Laboratory. He died in 1950.

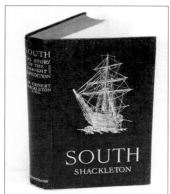

South by E H Shackleton first published in November 1919 (Tim Burr)

THE BLUE PLAQUE TO LIONEL GREENSTREET, A BRIXHAM RESIDENT AND THE LAST SURVIVOR OF SHACKLETON'S *ENDURANCE* EXPEDITION

POST CODE: TQ5 9NE

Commander Lionel Greenstreet, the First Officer on Shackleton's *Endurance* Expedition, retired to a bungalow he designed on Holwell Road, Brixham. He was the last survivor of the Expedition when he died in March 1979 at the age of 89. Caroline Alexander in her landmark book *The Endurance* quite rightly stated that '...it bankrupts the imagination to try to conceive that a man who sailed with Shackleton on the barquentine *Endurance* would live to see others walk on the moon'.

The last three survivors of the Endurance Expedition in 1970, Able Seaman Walter How, First Officer Lionel Greenstreet and cook Charles Green, photographed on 21 October 1970 at the commissioning of the new Survey Ship HMS Endurance in Portsmouth (Grace Turzig)

Greenstreet's house on Holwell Road is now a dental surgery but the owner has appropriately marked the connection with photos in the reception area and the Torbay Civic Society has placed a blue plaque on the wall. He lived here until he moved in later life to be closer to family in Sussex.

The blue plaque on Holwell Road, Brixham (Tim Burr)

Lionel Greenstreet was the last man to be recruited to *Endurance*. He was in Scotland the day before the ship sailed from Plymouth. The skipper Frank Worsley recommended him to Shackleton when the original choice of First Officer was called up for active service. When he arrived on board ship he was immediately given the job and given 30 minutes to get his kit together before the ship sailed!

In his diary Greenstreet wrote:

'August 8th Arrived Plymouth 7am and proceeded down to Endurance which was lying alongside at Millbay docks. Dirty morning with wind and rain. Everything in a muddle aboard getting stores various gear aboard her. ...12 (noon) cast off wharf getting a good send off from the people down to see her away. All hands mustered and returned cheers. Proceeded to anchorage in Cawsand Bay. Sir Ernest and various others leaving in the launch before getting outside...

August 9th 4am Hove up anchor and got underway'

Greenstreet proved to be an excellent choice; competent, loyal and cheerful. When later asked how they all survived such a gruelling experience, he answered with one word 'Shackleton'!

In 1960, Greenstreet was interviewed by *The Torquay Herald Express* about his *Endurance* experiences when the ship sank. 'I shall never forget the end when it came. Her timbers exploded like a machine gun barrage, her deck was crushed and her spars split like matchwood'. On the sea journey to Elephant Island he said: 'We rowed for our lives and by this time we were in a pretty bad shape. Our unremitting exposure to the elements and lack of food had reduced us to a pitiable condition'.

Greenstreet with 'breath icicles' photographed by Frank Hurley in September 1915 (SPRI)

During his retirement from the Royal Naval Reserve in Torquay he frequently lectured on his experiences in the Antarctic. He maintained a rather breezy and caustic sense of humour, and delighted in telling the newspaper which mistakenly printed his obituary in 1964 that it was premature and he was still very much alive!

THE QUEST EXPEDITION

1921 - 22

THE CAIRN TO SHACKLETON OVERLOOKING GRYTVIKEN HARBOUR
BY HUBERT WILKINS (SPRI)

SHACKLETON'S LAST EXPEDITION SETS SAIL FROM PLYMOUTH

Quest leaves Plymouth Sound, 24 September 1921. Shackleton can be seen, suited, just to the left of the funnel. The cinematograph is being operated by Bee Mason to his right, next to the ship's weather station. As a ship of the Royal Yacht Squadron, Quest was entitled to fly the white ensign at her stern (from The Graphic 1 October 1921)

After a number of unsuccessful ventures in Britain, Sir Ernest Shackleton was drawn back to the Antarctic. He was keen to return to southern waters in the company of some of his old expedition comrades. He took with him Frank Wild as Commander, Worsley as Sailing Master, Macklin as Surgeon (who incidentally had attended a school in Mannamead, Plymouth, as a boy) and Hussey as meteorologist. The expedition's aims were not fully clear although he had the notion of circumnavigating the continent and carrying out oceanographic work. The ship he used was called *Quest* and it was not in the best of condition. Several repairs had to be made on the journey to South Georgia and these must have added to the strains on Shackleton's health. On reaching South Georgia Shackleton suffered a massive heart attack during the night and died. Prophetically, and poetically, the last entry in his diary written the evening before was:

'In the darkening twilight I saw a lone star hover, gem like above the bay'...

Quest against the backdrop of Plymouth Hoe (Western Morning News) Inset of Ernest Shackleton, on the right, with J Q Rowett one of the main backers of the expedition, and a fellow old boy of Dulwich College, London.

Rare set of slides and viewer from the Quest Expedition (Tim Burr)

The ship sailed from Plymouth on Saturday 24 September 1921. Shackleton wrote in his diary:

'At last we are off. The last of the cheering crowded boats have turned, the sirens on shore and sea are still, and in the calm hazy dusk on a glassy sea we move on the long quest.'

The ship returned to Plymouth, anchoring in Cawsand Bay on 16 September 1922 and was met by J Q Rowett one of the main backers of the expedition. The ship naturally had a sad return without 'the Boss' who, on his wife's instructions, was buried on the island of South Georgia.

Shackleton once said: 'I go exploring because I like it and because it is my job. One goes once and then one gets the fever and can't stop going'.

Berth board for 'Quest'.

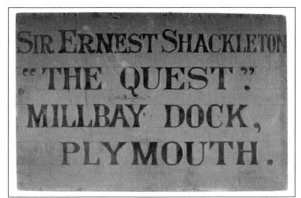

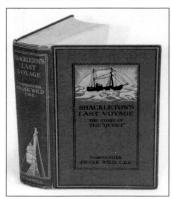

Shackleton's Last Voyage by Frank Wild (1923) (Tim Burr)

SELECT BIBLIOGRAPHY AND SOURCES

Discovery
T V Hodgson papers in SPRI
E Wilson 'Diary of the Discovery Expedition' Blandford 1966
Reports and Transactions of Devonshire Association 1927
R F Scott 'The Voyages of the Discovery' Smith Elder 1905
D Yelverton 'Antarctica Unveiled' University of Colorado 2000
J Debenham Back 'The Quiet Land' Bluntisham 1992
Shackleton et al 'The South Polar Times' Bonham 2002 reprint
Nimrod
E H Shackleton 'The Heart of the Antarctic' Heinemann 1909
Shackleton & MacKenna 'An Irishman in Antarctica' Lilliput 2002
Terra Nova
H Ludlam 'Captain Scott' Foulsham 1965
R F Scott 'Scott's Last Expedition' Smith Elder 1913
A Johnson 'Scott of the Antarctic and Cardiff' UCCP 1984
E R G R Evans 'South with Scott' Collins 1924
Fred Parsons unpublished memoir
R Priestley 'Antarctic Adventure' Fisher Unwin 1914
M Hooper 'The Longest Winter' Murray 2010
K Lambert 'Hell with a Capital H' Pimlico 2002
G Taylor 'With Scott:The Silver Lining' Smith Elder 1916
Francis Davies 'With Scott before the Mast' unpublished
P Keohane Diary SPRI
M Smith 'Great Endeavour' Collins 2010
The Sphere Magazine 24 May 1913
Max Jones 'The Last Great Quest' Oxford 2003
D James 'Scott of the Antarctic' Convoy publications 1948
Endurance
C Alexander 'The Endurance' Bloomsbury 1998
E H Shackleton 'South' Heinemann 1919
Thomson 'Elephant Island and Beyond' Bluntisham 2003
L Greenstreet Diary SPRI
Quest
F Wild 'Shackleton's Last Voyage' Cassell 1923
The Graphic Magazine 1 October 1921

Acknowledgements

Many of the pictures used in this book are reproduced courtesy of The Scott Polar Research Institute at the University of Cambridge. They are marked (SPRI) at the end of each caption. The source of other pictures is also given with the caption. All those without a given source are by the author or from his collection.

A number of people have given me considerable support and advice in writing this book and some have kindly loaned me material. I thank them all. They are: Bob Headland, Gill Poulter, Linda Noble, Heather Lane, Lucy Martin, Shirley Sawtell, Jane Chafer, Sarah O'Leary, Seamus Taaffe, Denis Wilkins, David Wilson, Mike Tarver, John Killingbeck, Tim Burr, Barry Chandler, Nigel Overton, Peter Paisley, Rob Glenning, Joy Watts, Grace Turzig, Jean Scholar, Peter Warren, Ian Howick, Richard Greenstreet, Graham Collyer. Apologies if I have missed anyone.

I should also like to acknowledge the assistance given to me by the following institutions: Plymouth City Museum, Torquay Museum, Plymouth Marine Biological Association, Discovery Point Dundee, Athy Heritage Centre Ireland, Scott Polar Research Institute and Stoke Damerel Community College.

I should especially like to thank Rob Stephenson and his magnificent Low Latitude Gazetter (available at www.antarctic-circle.org) for giving me the idea to research Devon's connections to the Heroic Age and to both the Vice Chancellor of the University of Plymouth, Professor Wendy Purcell and Sir Ranulph Fiennes for their support. Finally, of course, thanks to my wife Andrea for her constant patience and support.

Captain Scott's snow goggles (Discovery Point Museum)

A LIST OF LOCAL INSTITUTIONS WITH PRESENT DAY CONNECTIONS TO POLAR EXPLORATION

Education Through Expeditions is a community interest company, based at the University of Plymouth, which aims to provide educators with current and innovative distance-learning resources to support climate change education. It is headed by experienced Plymouth-based polar explorer, Antony Jinman.   Website: www.etelive.org

PML Plymouth Marine Laboratory   With the polar regions featuring strongly in its work, **Plymouth Marine Laboratory** is recognised internationally in delivering world-class integrated science addressing the interactions between the marine environment and society to sustain marine ecosystems, their services and societal benefits.   Website: www.pml.ac.uk

   The **MBA** is a Learned Society and one of the UK's leading marine biological research institutes. Its mission is to promote scientific research into all aspects of life in the sea and to disseminate to the public the knowledge gained.   Website: www.mba.ac.uk

British Antarctic Survey — NATURAL ENVIRONMENT RESEARCH COUNCIL   Plymouth Hospitals **NHS** NHS Trust

The British Antarctic Survey Medical Unit has been part of Plymouth Hospitals NHS Trust since 1997. Each year it trains and deploys four doctors to Antarctic ships and the British scientific research stations. An all year round/24hr emergency advice system supports these staff in their work from Derriford Hospital in the City of Plymouth.

Plymouth

Plymouth City Museum on North Hill has nine permanent galleries where thousands of objects and artworks from world cultures can be viewed. In the gallery *Plymouth: Port and Place* there is a showcase of Polar artefacts. These include Scott's skis, the model of *Terra Nova* and other artefacts relating especially to Patrick Keohane and Fred Dailey.

Website: www.plymouth.gov.uk/museums

Torquay Museum on Babbacombe Road was founded in 1844 by the Torquay Natural History Society. There is a newly refurbished gallery dedicated to *Explorers* which features amongst others Frank Browning from the *Terra Nova* Expedition, and also Lt Col. Percy Harrison Fawcett.

Website: www.torquaymuseum.org

Scott Polar Research Institute
University of Cambridge

SPRI was founded in 1920, in Cambridge, as a memorial to Captain Robert Scott and his four companions. The Institute is the oldest international centre for polar research within a university. It has an extensive archive of diaries, records and photographs related to the 'Heroic Age' and SPRI has recently reopened its museum after major refurbishment.

Website: www.spri.ac.uk

University of Plymouth

The University of Plymouth has a mission to be '*the* enterprise university'. The University is built on a rich heritage dating back to 1862 when the School of Navigation was established in the City. The University houses Europe's largest Marine Institute and is one of the founding partners in the Peninsula College of Medicine and Dentistry.

Website: www.plymouth.ac.uk

Routes taken by sledge parties during the *Terra Nova* Expedition 1910-13 and *Fram* Expedition 1910-12

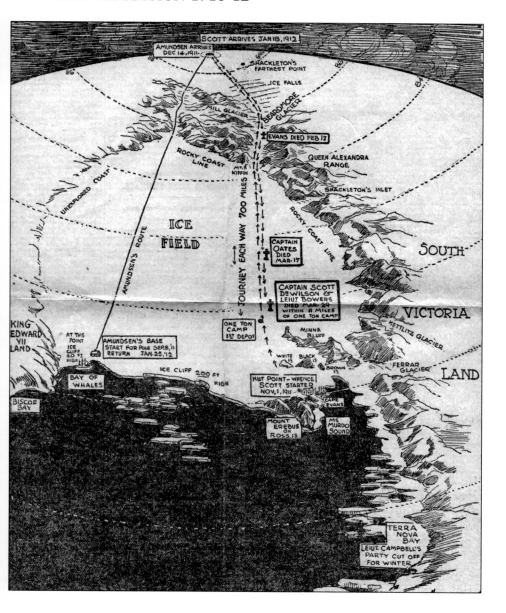